Love,

Grandma al Grandpa

Young

The Little Angels Book of Prayers

2016 First Printing This Edition

Text by Elena Pasquali
Illustrations copyright © 2008 Dubravka Kolanovic
Original edition published in English under the title "Prayers for Little Angels" by Lion Hudson plc, Oxford, England.
This edition copyright © 2016 Lion Hudson

Published in the United States and Canada by Paraclete Press, 2016.
ISBN 978-1-61261-853-1

Acknowledgments
All unattributed prayers are by Lois Rock, copyright © Lion Hudson.
Prayer by Mother Teresa used by permission.

Author Information
p. 10: Sarah Betts Rhodes (1824-1904)
p. 20: (top): From an old New England Sampler
p. 26: Mrs. Cecil Frances Alexander (1818-95)
p. 28: John Leland (1754-1841)
p. 30: Mother Teresa of Calcutta (1910-97)

10 9 8 7 6 5 4 3 2 1

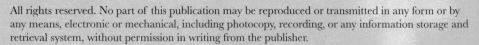

Published Paraclete Press
Brewster MA
www.paracletepress.com
Printed in Malaysia

The Little Angels Book of
Prayers

Elena Pasquali
Dubravka Kolanovic

PARACLETE PRESS
Brewster, Massachusetts

My angel friend

Angel of God, my guardian dear
To whom God's love commits me here,
Ever this day be at my side
To light and guard, to rule and guide.

Traditional

God has counted the stars in the heavens,
God has counted the leaves on the tree;
God has counted the children on earth:
I know God has counted me.

New day

Thank you, God in heaven,
For a day begun.
Thank you for the breezes,
Thank you for the sun.
For this time of gladness,
For our work and play,
Thank you, God in heaven,
For another day.

Traditional

Me

God, who made the earth,
The air, the sky, the sea,
Who gave the light its birth,
Careth for me.

God, who made the grass,
The flower, the fruit, the tree,
The day and night to pass,
Careth for me.

God, who made all things,
On earth, in air, in sea,
Who changing seasons brings,
Careth for me.

Sarah Betts Rhodes

Angels around me

Walking walking walking
An angel at my side;
Walking walking walking
An angel for my guide.
Walking walking walking
A journey without end;
Walking walking walking
An angel for my friend.

May the angels help me
when I cross the street –
keep me ever watchful
and direct my feet.

Being good

If I were an angel
then I would wear white
and only do things
that I knew to be right.

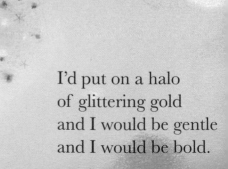

I'd put on a halo
of glittering gold
and I would be gentle
and I would be bold.

I'd flit through the world
on my soft feathered wings;
I'd speak words of kindness
and joyfully sing.

Helpfulness

May my hands be helping hands
For all that must be done
That fetch and carry, lift and hold
And make the hard jobs fun.

May my hands be clever hands
In all I make and do
With sand and dough and clay and things
With paper, paint and glue.

May my hands be gentle hands
And may I never dare
To poke and prod and hurt and harm
But touch with love and care.

Love

Love is giving, not taking,
mending, not breaking,
trusting, believing,
never deceiving,
patiently bearing
and faithfully sharing
each joy, every sorrow,
today and tomorrow.

Anonymous

Family

God bless all those that I love;
God bless all those that love me;
God bless all those that love those that I love,
And all those that love those that love me.

Anonymous

Dear God, bless all my family,
as I tell you each name;
and please bless each one differently
for no one's quite the same.

Home

Bless the window
Bless the door
Bless the ceiling
Bless the floor
Bless this place which is our home
Bless us as we go and come.

Let us take a moment
To give thanks for our food,
For friends around the table
And everything that's good.

World

For flowers that bloom about our feet,
Father, we thank Thee.
For tender grass so fresh and sweet,
Father, we thank Thee.
For the song of bird and hum of bee,
For all things fair we hear or see,
Father in heaven, we thank Thee.

For blue of stream and blue of sky,
Father, we thank Thee.
For pleasant shade of branches high,
Father, we thank Thee.
For fragrant air and cooling breeze,
For beauty of the blooming trees,
Father in heaven, we thank Thee.

Anonymous

Nature

All things bright and beautiful,
All creatures great and small,
All things wise and wonderful,
The Lord God made them all.

Mrs Cecil Frances Alexander

I think the butterfly
says her prayer
by simply fluttering
in the air.

I think the prayer
of the butterfly
just dances up
to God on high.

Goodnight

Lord, keep us safe this night,
Secure from all our fears;
May angels guard us while we sleep,
Till morning light appears.

John Leland

Now I lay me down to sleep,
I pray thee, Lord, thy child to keep;
Thy love to guard me through the night
And wake me in the morning light.

Traditional

I see the moon
And the moon sees me;
God bless the moon
And God bless me.

Traditional

We can do no great things,
Only small things with great love.

Mother Teresa of Calcutta